YOSEMITE

Photographs by William Neill
Text by Hannah Gosnell

Chronicle Books • San Francisco

COTTONWOODS AND YOSEMITE FALLS

At 2,425 feet, Yosemite Falls is the highest free-falling cascade in North America and the fifth highest in the world. There are three sections to this famous waterfall: Upper Fall (1,430 feet); Middle Cascades (675 feet); and Lower Fall (320 feet), which is alone more than twice as high as Niagara Falls.

As the seasons change, so does Yosemite Falls. In late summer and fall, it is often bone dry. Winter snows start the falls flowing again with meltwater from the high country. Ice cones frequently grow to be 300 feet high at the base of Upper Falls where freezing droplets of water collect.

With the spring runoff comes the most glorious time for Yosemite Falls. The huge quantity of falling water creates its own weather system, and visitors hiking to the base of Lower Falls can feel a temperature drop and increasing winds a quarter of a mile away.

LUPINE, WAWONA

There are more than 1,400 kinds of flowering plants in Yosemite National Park, and in the summer months Yosemite's meadows are transformed into natural wildflower gardens. One of the most common wildflowers found here is lupine, a member of the pea family.

The name lupine is derived from the Latin *lupus,* or wolf, because the plants were thought to "rob" the soil. It is now known that the contrary is true since legumes provide a source of nitrogen to soil. Still, many people remain suspicious of the plant since it contains alkaloids which are thought to be poisonous, causing a weak pulse, convulsions, and paralysis. The seeds, however, have been boiled and used for food by Native Americans.

There are over 80 species of lupines found in California, some 23 of which exist in Yosemite. Depending on the species, lupine grows in habitats ranging from dry rocky slopes to lush meadows, such as the one pictured here at Wawona.

MAMMOTH PEAK AND KUNA CREST
FROM TIOGA TARNS

The majestic alpine lakes that dot Yosemite's high country are largely the result of glacial activity, and the Tioga Tarns is no exception, having been gouged out by glaciers which occupied the Tuolumne Meadows region more than ten thousand years ago.

John Muir was the first one to attribute much of the Yosemite landscape to glaciers. His fascination with the power of ice is reflected in many of his writings, such as this one, which appeared in *The Californian* in 1880:

> Glaciers, back in their cold solitudes, work apart from men, exerting their tremendous energies in silence and darkness. Outspread, spirit-like, they brood above the predestined landscapes, work on unwearied through immeasurable ages, until, in the fullness of time, the mountains and valleys are brought forth, channels furrowed for the rivers, basins made for the lakes and meadows—then they shrink and vanish like summer clouds.

HALF DOME AND GLACIAL ERRATICS
NEAR OLMSTEAD POINT

Two million years ago, the first of three glacial advances took place in what is now known as Yosemite National Park. Hundreds, and in some places, thousands of feet of snow and ice blanketed the Sierra Nevada during these periods, the last of which ended only 10,000 years ago.

Glaciers, by definition, move or "flow" downhill, carving and sculpting the terrain beneath them. The scraping action of ice against rock often has a polishing effect on granite, resulting in patches of smooth, marble-like "glacial polish," as seen here at Olmstead Point.

Also seen here are "glacial erratics." Acting like conveyer belts, glaciers are capable of carrying large pieces of debris—dirt, rocks, even house-sized boulders. When temperatures rise, the glaciers melt and leave behind their cargo, often in improbable places. Geologic phenomena of this kind can be seen throughout the High Sierra.

VERNAL FALL WITH RAINBOW, MERCED RIVER

Vernal Fall was named in 1851 by Lafayette Bunnell, one of the first white men to enter Yosemite Valley. "The Vernal Fall I so named because of the cool, vernal spray in contrast at midday with summer heat, reminding me of an April shower, and because of the blue grass curiously growing among dark rocks and gay, dripping flowers, making it an eternal April to the ground."

Native Americans, noting this same phenomenon, called the waterfall "Yan-o-pah," or little cloud, because of the spray the old trail passed through. Indeed, the constant mist makes it wise to bring rain gear even on the sunniest days when visiting the Fall. This phenomenon, in conjunction with the California sunshine, results in continual rainbows around the waterfall, making it one of the most popular destinations in the Park. To reach the top of the 317-foot high Vernal Fall, one must hike up the Mist Trail, a steep, granite staircase carved into the rock in 1897.

CLEARING SUMMER STORM CLOUDS, GATES OF THE VALLEY

Although Yosemite National Park covers approximately 1,200 square miles, most of the Park's nearly 4 million annual visitors are attracted to Yosemite Valley, a seven-mile-long glacial canyon that boasts some of the most famous geologic features in the world. At the west end of the Valley—the narrowest part—are El Capitan, Bridalveil Falls, and Cathedral Rocks, known as the "Gates of the Valley."

John Muir wrote extensively about the Sierra, and Yosemite Valley was one of his favorite places. "No temple made with hands can compare with Yosemite. Every rock in its walls seems to glow with life. Some lean back in majestic repose; others, absolutely sheer or nearly so for thousands of feet, advance beyond their companions in thoughtful attitudes, giving welcome to storms and calms alike, seemingly aware, yet heedless, of everything going on about them."

CLOUD REFLECTIONS AND GRASSES, TUOLUMNE MEADOWS

In the summer, when crowds and heat characterize lower elevations, Tuolumne Meadows is a peaceful, cool haven at 8,600 feet above sea level. The largest subalpine meadow in the Sierra, Tuolumne is a land of granite domes, lakes, and wide open spaces. Some of the Park's highest peaks are in this region, soaring to heights of over 13,000 feet.

The Tuolumne River, fed by snowmelt and three glaciers upstream, begins its long journey to the lowlands in Tuolumne Meadows. On its way to Hetch Hetchy Reservoir, which supplies San Francisco with drinking water, the river winds its way through the Grand Canyon of Tuolumne, passing Glen Aulin High Sierra Camp, Waterwheel Falls, Muir Gorge, and Pate Valley.

During winter, it is not uncommon for the meadows to be buried under 20 feet of snow. Cars can generally pass through the areas during the summer months only, making· for a short visitation season.

GIANT SEQUOIAS, MARIPOSA GROVE

Yosemite National Park boasts three groves of giant sequoias, which are the largest living organisms on the planet. While the coast redwood, a close relative of the giant sequoia, is often taller, no tree can compare to the sequoia's incredible girth. A fully mature tree is normally 10 to 15 feet in diameter and 250 feet tall. Sequoias are also some of the oldest trees known, often living for 3,000 years or more.

Sequoia giganteum is a rare species, growing only on the western slope of the Sierra Nevada at elevations between 5,000 and 7,000 feet. To reproduce the sequoia requires the perfect combination of sunlight, water, and forest fire, which reduces the number of competing trees and adds minerals to the soil, so that only one in a billion seeds becomes a full-grown tree. There are approximately 75 groves of sequoias scattered throughout the Sierra.

For years loggers tried to harvest the wood from these monolithic trees, but it tended to be brittle, shattering into thousands of pieces when felled. Determined to utilize the wood, humans turned the majestic sequoias into toothpicks, pencils, grapevine stakes, and shingles until as recently as the 1950s.

JEFFREY PINE, SENTINEL DOME

This Jeffrey pine is one of the most famous trees in Yosemite, having attracted photographers for years with its gnarled wind-blown appearance and spectacular location on top of Sentinel Dome. Perhaps the most famous photograph was taken by Ansel Adams in 1940, when the tree was still alive. In 1976 and 1977, California suffered from extreme drought and the old Jeffrey died. Nonetheless, it retains its dramatic character.

The Jeffrey pine is frequently seen on stark granite domes throughout the Sierra, as it is one of the few species that has adapted to the harsh, exposed, arctic climate found on top of most high domes. John Muir commented on this particular tree, calling it "a sturdy storm-enduring mountaineer of a tree, living on sunshine and snow, maintaining tough health on this diet for perhaps more than a thousand years."

MAPLE LEAVES AND BOULDERS, YOSEMITE VALLEY

One of the most delightful autumn sights in Yosemite Valley is the changing colors of the bigleaf maple. Since the majority of trees in Yosemite are coniferous, or evergreen, it is rare to see bright colors unless one ventures into the cool, moist shady sections along the Merced River. There, one is surrounded by maple branches and falling leaves, and with sunlight filtering down every object appears as a different shade of yellow.

Fall in Yosemite is a time of shutting down for most plants and animals. As the Park empties of summer visitors, so do deciduous trees lose their leaves, in anticipation of freezing temperatures. In many ways, fall and winter are seasons of recovery for Yosemite. Trees and shrubs prepare for spring bloom, drinking up the moisture that has long been absent during the summer months, and meadows take a break from trampling feet under the protection of snow.

MERCED RIVER, WINTER, YOSEMITE VALLEY

Placid as it may seem, the Merced River is the main geologic feature responsible for the formation of Yosemite Valley. For ten million years it has been eroding away the granite bedrock, continuously cutting deeper. Not until relatively recently —two million years ago— did glaciers arrive to carve the already established river canyon to what is almost its present width and depth.

Originating in the High Sierra, the Merced tumbles through steep canyons, dropping thousands of feet and forming Nevada and Vernal Falls before it reaches the Valley. There it joins with Tenaya Creek and meanders peacefully for several miles before it begins another series of steep drops to the San Joaquin Valley far below.

It was a Spanish exploring party led by Sergeant Gabriel Moraga who named the river "El Rio de Nuestra Senora de la Merced" (The River of Our Lady of Mercy) in 1806, after having traveled more than forty miles without water.

EL CAPITAN AND MERCED RIVER, WINTER SUNSET, GATES OF THE VALLEY

The Yosemite Indians called this giant rock "To-to-kon-oolah." According to legend, two bear cubs fell asleep on a large, flat rock one day. As they slept, the rock grew to the clouds, leaving them stranded. When their mother discovered their predicament, she enlisted the help of all the other animals. The only one who could climb the steep, slippery wall to rescue the cubs was the inchworm, who chanted "Too-tock, too-tock, to-to-kon-oolah" on his way up.

Today El Capitan continues to challenge those who attempt to climb its sheer walls. Rock climbers from all over the world come to Yosemite to test themselves on the myriad routes lining the monolith, which is one of the largest exposed granite blocks in existence. With its cliff rising 3,000 feet above the Valley floor, and its peak 600 feet higher, El Capitan is one of the most famous landmarks in Yosemite National Park.

HALF DOME AND ELM TREE IN COOKE'S MEADOW

One of the most striking features in Yosemite is Half Dome, a giant monolith at the east end of Yosemite Valley. The most frequently asked question about Half Dome is "Where is the other half?" Actually, only a third of the dome is missing, and parts of it can be found in the rubble at the base of the cliff. Other bits of Half Dome were eroded and carried down-valley by running water and glaciers, and have been found by geologists in the Merced River Canyon as far down as the San Joaquin Valley where the river ends.

The sheer, 1,200-foot north face of Half Dome attracts rock climbers with its variety of challenging routes, and the rare and endangered peregrine falcon with its excellent nesting sites.

Native Americans called Half Dome "Tis-sa-ock" after a woman who was thought to have been turned to stone by the Great Spirit. According to legend, her tear-stained face can still be seen in the granite.

SUNSET REFLECTIONS, SPRING THAW, TENAYA LAKE

For thousands of years, what is now known as Tenaya Lake was a major landmark used by Miwok Indians traveling across the Sierra to trade with Mono Paiutes on the east side of the range. Native Americans called the lake "Py-wi-ock" or "Lake of the Glistening Rocks" for all the glacially polished domes and slabs in the area. It was the Tuolumne Glacier, more than ten thousand years ago, that was responsible for scouring the surrounding rocks and gouging out the basin in which the lake sits today.

Tenaya Lake is one of the largest lakes in Yosemite National Park, stretching one mile long and a half mile wide. Its present name comes from members of the Mariposa Battalion of 1851, who wanted to honor the Chief of the Yosemite Miwoks, Tenaya. Despite this gesture of respect, the Mariposa Battalion eventually drove the Yosemite Indians away to make room for pioneer settlements.

DOGWOOD BLOOMING ALONG MERCED RIVER, YOSEMITE VALLEY

The Pacific dogwood in bloom is one of the first signs of spring in Yosemite. As the waterfalls increase their velocity in early to mid-April, the creamy white blossoms begin to appear all over the Valley, especially in the moist, shady places along creeks and rivers.

The dogwood is unique among most hardwoods in that it carries out maximum photosynthesis in conditions which are only one-third of full sunlight. Thus it is often found growing at the foot of large conifers such as pines and giant sequoias, generally at elevations between 3,500 and 6,000 feet. While the conifers grow to be hundreds of feet tall, the dogwood is usually only 20 to 40 feet tall, with a slender trunk and spreading branches.

In the fall, the flowers develop into clusters of bright red berry-like fruits and the leaves are green, orange, or scarlet. While the berries are edible, they are bitter. Native Americans boiled the smooth, ashy gray bark for use as a laxative.

Compilation and text © 1993 Chronicle Books

Photos © William Neill

Printed in Singapore.

Design by Karen Pike.
Typography by T:H Typecast, Inc.

ISBN 0-8118-0277-9

Chronicle Books
275 Fifth Street
San Francisco, California 94103